D0101957

Test Paper B

Instructions:

- find a quiet place where you can sit down and complete the test paper undisturbed

- an adult will need to read the first 5 questions to you

- make sure you have all the necessary equipment to complete the test paper (a pencil, rubber, ruler and small mirror)

- read the questions carefully

- answer all the questions in this booklet

- go through and check your answers when you have finished the test paper

Time:

Take as long as necessary to complete the test paper.

Note to Parents:

Check how your child has done against the mark scheme in the Answers Booklet.

Test Paper B

Page	3	5	7	9	11	13	15	17	19	Max. Mark	**Actual Mark**
Score	....	....	....	....	....	....	....	....	....	30	....

First name   _____

Last name   _____

1 A pair of jeans costs £18. A coat costs £23 more.
How much does the coat cost? **Write your answer in box a.**

2 2 numbers are multiplied together to make 180.
Which 2 numbers could be multiplied together? **Write your 2 numbers in boxes b and c.**

3 A cuboid has 3 red faces and 1 blue face. The other faces are all yellow. How many faces of the cuboid are yellow? **Write your answer in box d.**

4 Write the number one thousand and ninety four. **Write it in box e.**

5 Circle the units you would use to measure your weight.

Now continue with the rest of the paper on your own.

1   a) £ | 41 | *(1 mark)* ☐
Q1

2   b) | 10 | c) | 18 | *(1 mark)* ☐
Q2

3   d) | 2 | faces   *(1 mark)* ☐
Q3

4   e) | 1094 | *(1 mark)* ☐
Q4

5   kilometres   millimetres   minutes

       (kilograms)   litres   *(1 mark)* ☐
Q5

Turn over

subtotal

6 Here are some signs.

| = | | × | | − |

Write a sign in each box to make this correct.

140 $=$ 2 $\times$ 70

(1 mark)

QE

7 How many 5p pieces are there in £1.50?

$3\ 0$ 5p pieces

(1 mark)

8 Look at these amounts. **Place them in order in the boxes below.**

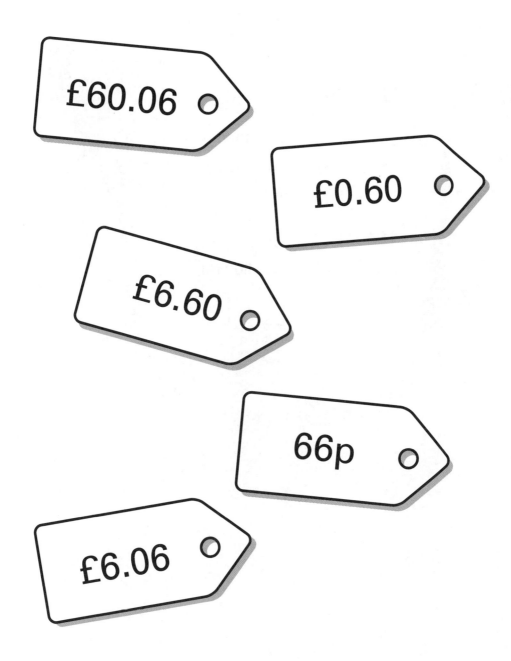

£60.06

£0.60

£6.60

66p

£6.06

| £60.06 | £6.60 | £6.06 | 66p | £0.60 |

most   **least**

(1 mark)

9 Shade this container to show 250 ml.

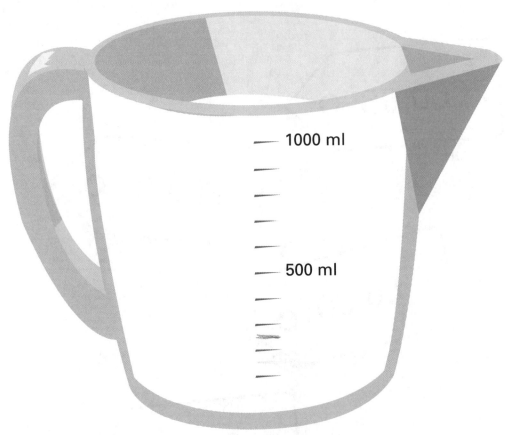

— 1000 ml

— 500 ml

(1 mark)

10 1

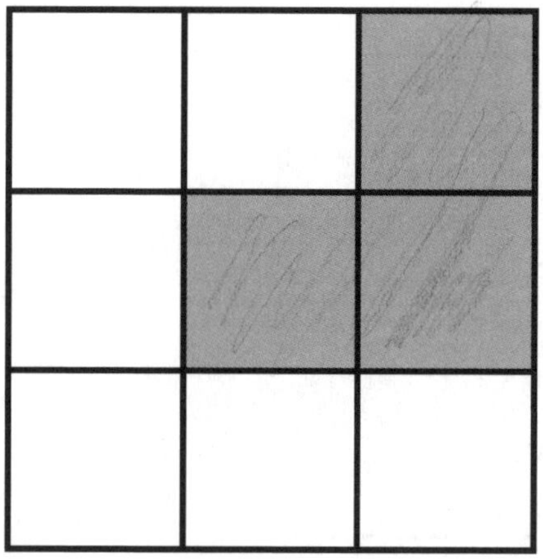

These grids are turned by a $\frac{1}{4}$ turn each time.

Shade in the squares in the last grid to complete the pattern.

2

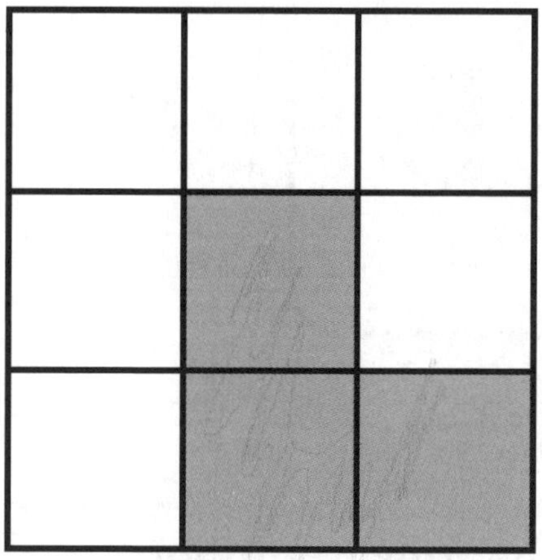

3

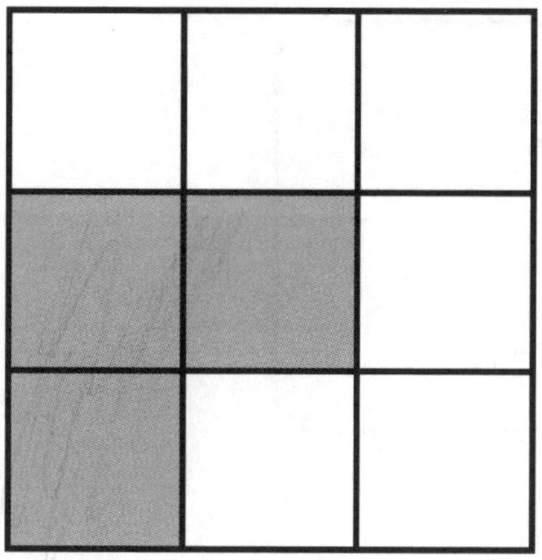

4

(1 mark)

11 Write the total.

74 + 116 = $\boxed{190}$

(1 mark)

12 Look at these cards.

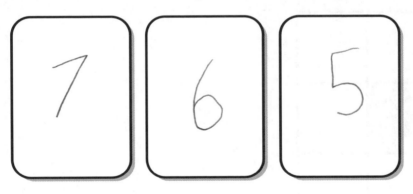

a) Use each card **once** to make the **largest** number.

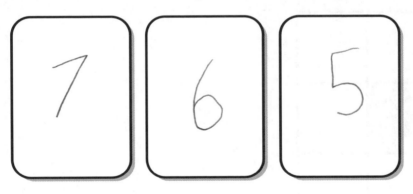

(1 mark)

b) Use each card **once** to make the **smallest even** number.

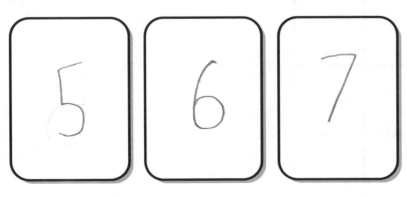

(1 mark)

13 George's baby bottle contains 100 ml of juice.

If he drinks $\frac{1}{4}$ of it, how much is left?

75 ml

(1 mark)

Q13

Spelling test results: Red group (marks out of 50)	
Javed	48
Chloe	32
Helen	24
Meera	39
Peter	43
Jilly	46
David	21

The children's spelling test results are shown on a bar chart. They received 1 mark for each correct spelling, but 2 scores have been mixed up.

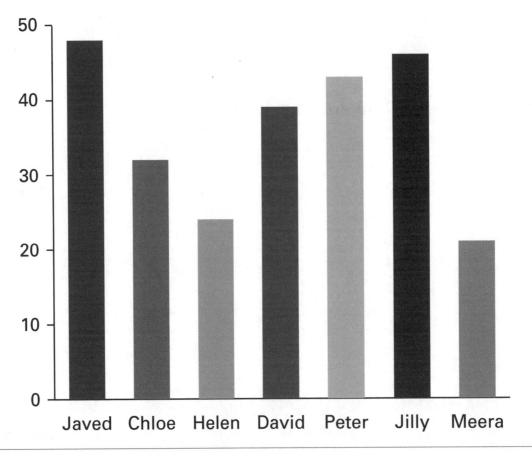

a) Whose scores are incorrect on the bar chart?

_____Meera_____ and _____David_____ *(1 mark)*

b) Who scored half the number of marks Javed got?

_____Helen_____ *(1 mark)*

c) How many **incorrect**
spellings did David have?   29   *(1 mark)*

15 Estimate the number marked by the arrow.

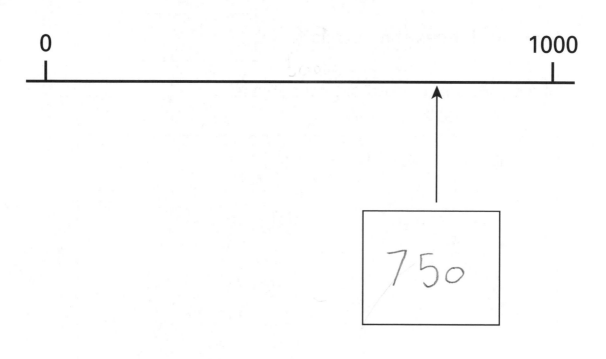

0   1000

750

Write the number in the empty box.   *(1 mark)*

Turn over

subtotal

16 Melanie has £20.

She buys an ice-cream and a cinema ticket.

How much does she have left?   £ ☐

Show how you worked out your answer.

She uses £3.80
20 + 3 = 17
£17 − 80p =

(1 mark)

17 Fill in the correct number.

$$237 + \boxed{421} = 658$$

(1 mark)

18 Draw the reflection of this shape in the mirror line.

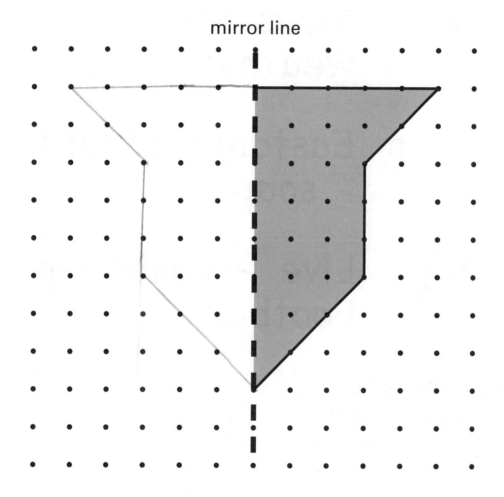

mirror line

(1 mark)

TV1

7.00 pm **Cartoons - kids' funtime**

7.35 pm **News and weather**

8.10 pm **Eastdale Street - soap**

8.45 pm **Live Premiership Football**

How many minutes does
'News and weather' last? ☐ minutes   *(1 mark)*

20 In his shopping bag, Tariq has 2 kg of potatoes, 500 g of carrots and $1\frac{1}{2}$ kg of onions.

What does his shopping bag weigh? ☐ kg

(1 mark)

21

	has 3 digits	does not have 3 digits
odd	173	61
even		1004

Write these numbers in the correct place on the chart.

7939   240   637

(1 mark)

Turn over

22 Write a number in each box to make this correct.

$$600 \div 3 = \boxed{} \times \boxed{}$$

(1 mark)

23 Write the answer.

$$500 - 37 = \boxed{}$$

(1 mark)

24 Write the missing numbers in this sequence.

1018 1008 $\boxed{}$ 988 $\boxed{}$ 968 958

(1 mark)

25 Carl worked out the correct answer to **84 ÷ 6**.

His answer was **14**.

Show how he could have worked out his answer.

(1 mark)

26 Amrita is thinking of a number.

When I double my number and add 7 my answer is 23.

What number is she thinking of? ☐ *(1 mark)*

27 Match each addition to its answer.

One has been done for you.

| 30 + 30 + 30 |

| 25 + 25 + 25 + 25 + 25 |

| 70 + 70 + 70 + 70 |

| 200 |

| 125 |

| 135 |

| 90 |

| 190 |

| 280 |

(1 mark)

END OF TEST

KEY STAGE 1
Levels 1–3

Answers,
Mark Scheme
and
Advice Booklet

Maths

Answers

Answers, Mark Scheme and Advice Booklet

This booklet provides advice on how to use the tests, as well as supplying the answers and the mark schemes for each of the test papers.

On page 3 of this booklet, there is a grid to record your child's marks in and a guide showing how these marks relate to levels.

Contents

Understanding the SATs

What are the SATs?
SATs are taken by pupils at the end of Year 2 in English and Mathematics. Teacher assessments will form the main part of the child's result. However, National Tests will validate the teacher's own assessment.

What do the tests assess in your child?
All children study the National Curriculum from Year 1. At the end of Year 2, the tests will assess your child's knowledge, skills and understanding in the programmes of study that they have followed from Year 1.

In Mathematics, the Programme of Study covers four areas or Attainment Targets:

Mathematics 1:   Using and applying mathematics

Mathematics 2:   Number and algebra

Mathematics 3:   Space, shape and measures

Mathematics 4:   Handling data

Levels of Attainment
When your child's Mathematics papers are marked, the correct marks are collated to give your child an overall score. This score is then matched to a National Curriculum level.

The government target for pupils at the end of Year 2 is to achieve Level 2. Some pupils will be working below this level and achieve Level 1, whilst other pupils will be working above the expected level and achieve Level 3.

Preparing your child for the Tests

These Practice Papers are designed to prepare your child for the National Tests by giving them the confidence of knowing the sort of questions they will experience.

In order for your child to achieve their full potential, the National Tests take place in school in a relaxed, informal atmosphere, with no time limit. You will need to recreate this atmosphere at home to give your child the best chance.

How will these Practice Papers help?
These Practice Papers will be just like the National Tests your child will do at school. They will give you an indication of your child's strengths and weaknesses and how you can help them.

How can you improve your child's score?
- Mark the papers.
- Look at what your child got wrong and talk it through with them.
- Let your child do the test again.
- Remember – keep practising the things they get wrong. For example, if they find subtraction difficult, give them plenty of practice.
- Try to encourage your child not to throw away marks, by reading a question carefully and checking their answer.

Marking the Practice Papers

1   Marking the practice papers is quite simple. Just use the answers provided in this booklet for each test.

2   Make sure your child has completed the relevant test.

3   Add up the marks on the paper. Each test is marked out of 30.

4   Write the marks in the corresponding table below.

	Paper A	Paper B	Paper C
Score (out of 30)			

Finding the level

Paper A

Add up your child's total score for the test out of the maximum of 30 marks. Then refer to the table below to find the level and grade.

Number of marks	0–4	5–6	7–12	13–18	19–30
Level	No level	Level 1	Level 2C	Level 2B	Level 2A

If your child achieved Level 2A in Test Paper A, then they can try either or both of the Level 3 papers.

Papers B and C

Add up your child's total score for the test out of the maximum of 30 marks. Then refer to the table below to find whether they have achieved Level 3.

Number of marks	0–10	11–30
Level	Level 3 not achieved	Level 3 achieved

In school your child would only take one Level 3 paper. However, two tests are provided here for additional practice at home.

Success in these tests is a good indication of success in the actual SATs but, of course, it cannot be a guarantee.

Paper A – Answers

1) 8 *(1 mark)*

   Note to parent – *This question aims to encourage your child to subtract mentally while recognising that the wording 'less than' suggests a subtraction operation.*

2) 20 children *(1 mark)*

   Note to parent – *Your child needs to be able to count in 5s or recall facts from the x5 table. This question puts the multiplication operation in a real-life context.*

3) *(1 mark)*

   Note to parent – *An understanding of the properties of 2D shapes is needed. Your child should be aware that triangles have 3 sides and there are lots of different types of triangle. You could look for different triangles in the environment – e.g. road signs, paving patterns etc.*

4) 20 ÷ 5 *(1 mark)*

   Note to parent – *This question encourages your child to work out each of the 4 operations of addition, subtraction, multiplication and division. Division facts are related to multiplication facts and your child should know that 20 ÷ 5 can be derived from 4 × 5.*

5) *(1 mark)*

   Note to parent – *Children should be able to read simple scales on rulers, weighing scales, clocks and capacity measures. The most effective way for children to learn to read scales is through practical activities – e.g. cooking, craft activities and telling the time.*

6) 14 stickers *(1 mark)*

   Note to parent – *Your child should be able to recall number bonds (numbers which add up or subtract) to 20. They may also use visual clues to add on, starting with the largest number.*

7) *(1 mark)*

   Note to parent – *Encourage your child to use language associated with shape and the names of shapes – e.g. long, short, corner, hexagon, right angle etc. Look for shapes in the environment and encourage pattern making as an art activity.*

8) Any 2 pairs of numbers that total 19 – e.g. 10 + 9, 2 + 17 etc. All 4 numbers must be different to achieve the marks. *(2 marks)*

   Note to parent – *As mentioned in question 6, your child needs to be secure with number bonds to 20. You can play games such as number ping-pong with a starting number – e.g. 15. You each take turns to say the numbers which add up – e.g. 8 & 7, 9 & 6.*

9) 8p *(1 mark)*

   Note to parent – *Encourage your child to become familiar with real coins, making totals and finding change. This question involves adding on from 15 to get to 23 and an understanding of 'how much more'.*

10) 22 *(1 mark)*

   Note to parent – *Your child should look for pairs of numbers that make 10. Then add on from the largest number.*

11) 23 = 47 – 24 or 23 = 67 – 44, or any numbers that have a difference of two. *(1 mark)*

   Note to parent – *The first missing digit must be greater by 2 than the second missing digit. Your child should use their knowledge of place value in recognising that the tens digits needs to have a difference of 2.*

12) 47 satsumas *(1 mark)*

   Note to parent – *Counting in tens is a very useful and efficient activity in problem solving. It helps with children's understanding of place value and the number system.*

13) 54, 49, 44, **39**, 34, 29, **24** *(1 mark)*

   Note to parent – *Your child should recognise that the units digits are alternating between 4 and 9, and the sequence is counting back through the tens numbers. There are limitless numbers of sequences that can be made to practise this type of activity.*

14) The line should be 14 cm long.   *(1 mark)*
    Note to parent – *It is important that your child can accurately use a ruler marked in centimetres. Ensure they start measuring and drawing from zero. Children can do measuring around the home with rulers, tape measures and string. They should be able to begin to estimate lengths and order the size of objects.*

15) 4 and 12 or 17 and 9   *(1 mark)*
    Note to parent – *This question requires an understanding of the term 'difference' between 2 numbers and that your child can count on from the smaller number or back from the larger number.*

16) 40, 10, 90 (all 3 numbers must be circled)
    (1 mark)
    Note to parent – *Your child should be able to recognise numbers divisible by 10 as those which have a zero as the units digit.*

17) 3 children   *(1 mark)*
    Note to parent – *Pictograms are a common way of displaying information in a visual way. Your child can carry out surveys at home about favourite pets, fruit, TV programmes etc. and display the information as a pictogram.*

18) 103   *(1 mark)*
    Note to parent – *Your child should have an understanding of the value of each digit in 3-digit numbers. They could make cards with individual digits on them, then make hundreds numbers and order them. They could also collect 3-digit numbers from car registration plates and order them.*

19)   *(1 mark)*
    Note to parent – *Your child should know that a rectangle has 2 pairs of equal sides. A square is also a rectangle where both pairs of sides are the same.*

20) a) 7 marbles   *(1 mark)*
    b) 2p   *(1 mark)*
    Note to parent – *Your child should be able to count in 5s and recall facts in the ×5 table. This question also involves calculating the remainder from a division problem involving money.*

21) 12   *(1 mark)*
    Note to parent – *Your child should be able to add 8 on from 13. They may recognise that 9 is 1 more than 8 so the other number has to be 1 less than 13.*

22) 18   *(1 mark)*
    Note to parent – *Knowing doubles of numbers up to 20 is useful in addition problems.*

23) a) 1, 5, 9, **13**, 17, **21**, 25   *(1 mark)*
    b) 26, 22, **18**, **14**, 10, **6**, 2   *(1 mark)*
    All the numbers are needed for each mark.
    Note to parent – *Encourage your child to look at all the numbers in the sequences to establish a pattern. Both patterns involve jumps of 4.*

24)   *(1 mark)*
    Note to parent – *Encourage your child to read both analogue (dial) and digital clocks and associate times with events – e.g. start and end of school, favourite TV programme, bedtime etc. Ensure the minute hand is longer than the hour hand when drawing on analogue clocks.*

25) 38   *(1 mark)*
    Note to parent – *Your child should recognise the language 'less than' as subtraction. They may count back 10 first, then the 2. A number line is useful for visualising counting back.*

26) 17 people   *(1 mark)*
    Note to parent – *This is a real-life problem requiring the operation of subtraction. Encourage your child to solve real-life problems involving all 4 operations of number.*

27)   *(1 mark)*
    Note to parent – *Venn diagrams are a way of representing information with 2 or more variables. This question also requires an understanding of odd and even numbers.*

Paper B – Answers

1) £41 *(1 mark)*
   Note to parent – *Your child will have developed mental strategies for adding two 2-digit numbers. They may start with the larger number, then partition the other number into tens and units, then add each in turn – i.e. 23 + 10 = 33, 33 + 8 = 41.*

2) 90 & 2, 6 & 30, 1 & 180, etc. *(1 mark)*
   Any 2 numbers that multiply together to make 180.
   Note to parent – *Your child may use known facts – e.g. 9 × 2 = 18, so 90 × 2 = 180. As a practice activity you could give your child a number and ask them to find as many ways of making it using all 4 operations.*

3) 2 faces *(1 mark)*
   Note to parent – *It is important that your child can visualise 3D shapes. They should be aware of how many faces regular solid shapes have.*

4) 1094 *(1 mark)*
   Note to parent – *At Level 3, your child should be able to recognise the vocabulary of the number system and write corresponding numbers with 4 digits. They should understand the value of each digit in a number and in this number know that a zero is needed as the hundreds digit.*

5) kilograms *(1 mark)*
   Note to parent – *Your child should have experience of the different units used to measure length, capacity, mass (weight) and time. Ensure they have plenty of practical experience around the home and when playing.*

6) 140 = 2 × 70 *(1 mark)*
   Note to parent – *In this equation the answer is shown first. Your child should be familiar with this layout as well as the more conventional equation where the answer comes at the end.*

7) 30 5p pieces *(1 mark)*
   Note to parent – *Your child may count in 5s up to 150 or recognise that there are three 5s in 15 so there must be thirty 5s in 150. Basic multiplication facts are very useful for solving a range of problems.*

8) £60.06, £6.60, £6.06, 66p, £0.60 *(1 mark)*
   Note to parent – *All values must be in the correct order to achieve the mark. This question requires an understanding of place value and decimal notation for money. Playing shops at home is a fun way for children to learn the value of coins, finding totals and working out change.*

9) *(1 mark)*
   Note to parent – *Show your child that each mark is 100 ml and 50 ml is halfway between two. Practical experience when cooking is the best way for your child to learn about weighing and measuring.*

10) *(1 mark)*
   Note to parent – *Your child may find it easier to rotate the page to see how the pattern changes with each $\frac{1}{4}$. They can learn about $\frac{1}{2}$ and $\frac{1}{4}$ turns by making maps, following directions etc. when playing.*

11) 190 *(1 mark)*
   Note to parent – *Encourage your child to see pairs of numbers that can be added easily – e.g. 6 + 4 – and start with the bigger number: 116 + 4 = 120, 120 + 70 = 190.*

12) a) 765 *(1 mark)*
    b) 576 *(1 mark)*
   Note to parent – *Again, your child needs to understand the value of each digit in a 3-digit number. They also need to know that an even number must end in 0, 2, 4, 6 or 8.*

13) 75 ml *(1 mark)*
   Note to parent – *Your child should be able to work out a $\frac{1}{4}$ of an amount by halving and halving again. At Level 3, they need to be able to solve word problems, identifying what operation is needed.*

14) Meera and David *(1 mark)*
    Helen *(1 mark)*
    29 *(1 mark)*
   Note to parent – *At Level 3, children need to extract and interpret information displayed in bar charts, lists and tables. This is a vertical bar chart. Bar charts may also be orientated horizontally.*

15) Any number between 750 and 850.   *(1 mark)*
    Note to parent – *Using unmarked number lines enables your child to gain a better understanding of the number system, while estimating and approximating numbers up to 1000.*

16) £16.20   *(1 mark)*
    Note to parent – *This is a multi-step problem which requires your child to add the value of the ice-cream and cinema ticket, then subtract this amount from £20. Encourage them to write each step of the solution.*

17) 421   *(1 mark)*
    Note to parent – *When your child is faced with an equation with a missing number, they will need to use their understanding of inverse operations. In this question, they may count on from 237 to 658 on a number line or subtract 237 from 658.*

18)   *(1 mark)*
    Note to parent – *Use a mirror to help your child see where the mirror line or line of symmetry is. Look for other symmetrical shapes around the home.*

19) 35 minutes   *(1 mark)*
    Note to parent – *Ensure your child understands how to read times, calculate periods of time and solve problems. TV guides and timetables are very useful everyday ways of practising these skills.*

20) 4 kg   *(1 mark)*
    Do not accept $3\frac{1}{2}$ kg and 500 g.
    Note to parent – *Your child needs to recognise that 500 g is equivalent to $\frac{1}{2}$ kg. Take items from the kitchen and ask them to add the total weight. Weigh loose fruits and vegetables in the supermarket on the scales.*

21)   *(1 mark)*

	has 3 digits	does not have 3 digits
odd	173 **637**	61 **7939**
even	**240**	1004

Note to parent – *All 3 numbers must be in the correct boxes to gain the mark. Carroll diagrams are a way of representing information with 2 variables.*

22) 20 & 10, 200 & 1, 4 & 50 etc.   *(1 mark)*
    Any 2 numbers that multiply together to make 200.
    Note to parent – *Your child needs to work out the division first, then identify 2 numbers to multiply together to make 200. They may use known facts – e.g. 2 × 10 = 20 so 20 × 10 = 200, 4 × 5 = 20 so 4 × 50 = 200.*

23) 463   *(1 mark)*
    Note to parent – *Your child may round the 37 up to 40, then subtract to give 500 – 40 = 460. Then they will need to add the 3 back on, so 460 + 3 = 463. They may round 37 down to 30, so 500 – 30 = 470, then subtract the further 7, 470 – 7 = 463.*

24) 1018 1008 **998** 988 **978** 968 958   *(1 mark)*
    Note to parent – *This question aims to encourage your child to explore numbers beyond 1000. They should identify that the sequence is going down in tens. Care is needed when crossing the hundreds boundary from 1008 to 998.*

25) A complete and correct method must be recorded for the mark to be awarded.*(1 mark)*
    Note to parent – *Your child may show counting in 6s – 6, 12, 18, 24 etc. They may make 84 marks and separate them into 6 groups of 14. They may do a repeated subtraction 84 – 6 = 78, 78 – 6 = 72 etc. or show the inverse operation of 6 × 14 = 84.*

26) 8   *(1 mark)*
    Note to parent – *Your child needs to work backwards from the total; 23 – 7 = 16, 16 ÷ 2 = 8. Try to make up some of these puzzles when in the car or walking to school.*

27)   *(1 mark)*

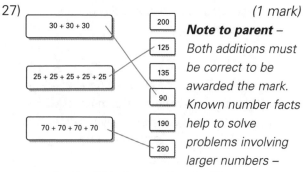

Note to parent – *Both additions must be correct to be awarded the mark. Known number facts help to solve problems involving larger numbers – e.g. 4 × 7 = 28 helps to solve 4 × 70.*

Paper C – Answers

1) 27   *(1 mark)*

Note to parent – *Your child should be able to recall number bonds to 20 and add smaller numbers mentally.*

2) 1 hour 30 minutes or 90 minutes   *(1 mark)*

Note to parent – *Using a film or TV guide sets challenges and problems for your child in real-life contexts so that they develop an understanding of time.*

3) 23   *(1 mark)*

Note to parent – *Your child should recognise the term 'difference' as subtraction. They may count on from the smaller number or subtract the tens and units separately.*

4) 5p   *(1 mark)*

Note to parent – *This is a simple 2-step problem involving multiplication and subtraction. Encourage your child to use money in shops for buying small items so that they familiarise themselves with real-life money situations.*

5)   *(1 mark)*

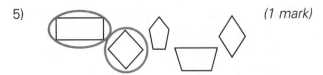

Note to parent – *Make a right-angle measurer from a corner of a piece of paper and encourage your child to look for right angles on shapes around the home.*

6) 470   *(1 mark)*

Note to parent – *In order to solve this problem, your child should find the difference between the 2 numbers, halve it, then add this on to the smaller number.*

7) 37   *(1 mark)*

Note to parent – *Your child will have developed a strategy for subtracting a 2-digit number while crossing the tens boundary. They may round 56 to 60, subtract this from 93, then add the extra 4 they subtracted. 93 – 60 = 33, 33 + 4 = 37. Encourage your child to check their answer by adding again, 56 + 37 = 93.*

8) 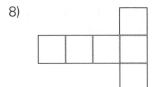   *(1 mark)*

Note to parent – *You can dismantle cereal packets etc. to show the 'nets' of 3D shapes. It is important that your child can visualise 3D shapes from a 2D representation.*

9)   *(1 mark)*

Note to parent – *Scales can be represented vertically, horizontally or curved, as on bathroom scales. Ensure your child is familiar with a range of scales for measuring capacity and weight (mass).*

10) a) seafood and spicy sausage   *(1 mark)*
    b) 34 children   *(1 mark)*

Note to parent – *Pictograms are a common way of representing information. Your child should identify that $\frac{3}{4}$ of the circle represents 3 children, $\frac{1}{2}$ of the circle represents 2 children and $\frac{1}{4}$ represents 1 child before they begin to answer the questions. Look out for pictograms in newspapers and magazines.*

11) 507, **398**, 396, **393**, 391, **308**, 268   *(1 mark)*

Note to parent – *Your child should have a secure understanding of place value of 3-digit numbers when working at Level 3.*

12) 58 cm   *(1 mark)*

Note to parent – *This is a similar calculation to question 7, but puts subtraction in a practical, real-life context. Your child should use a similar strategy for solving it.*

13)   *(1 mark)*

Note to parent – *A mirror can be used to help locate where the lines of symmetry should be drawn.*

14) 320 cm or 3 m 20 cm   *(1 mark)*

Note to parent – *Your child may do repeated addition of 80 + 80 + 80 + 80 or use 4 × 8 = 32, so 4 × 80 = 320. Encourage them to show the answer as metres and centimetres.*

15) 18   (1 mark)
   Note to parent – Your child may count in 5s up to
   90, or know that there are twenty 5s in 100 so
   there must be 2 less in 90.

16) 894   (1 mark)
   Note to parent – Your child may first be tempted
   to put 948 as the answer, but remind them to
   work out the numbers before 900 also. This
   question tests their understanding of place value
   of 3-digit numbers.

17) 38 and 32   (1 mark)
   Note to parent – Your child should look for 2 units
   numbers which add up to 10 – e.g. 3 and 7, 2 and
   8. Then they should look for the value of the tens
   numbers to make their final total.

18) Any 6-sided shape that is different from those
   shown. All sides must join. Do not award the
   mark if an orientation of shape already shown
   is drawn.   (1 mark)
   Note to parent – Vertices (corners) do not need
   to touch the dots to award the mark. Ensure your
   child knows the number of sides of these 2D
   shapes: circle, triangle, square, rectangle,
   pentagon, hexagon, octagon.

19) a) plants and cakes   (1 mark)
   b) £48 (accept £47 or £49)   (1 mark)
   Note to parent – This is a horizontal bar chart
   representing information. Your child needs to
   interpret the scale and estimate the values. They
   could carry out a survey at home about favourite
   fruits, TV programmes etc. and make their own
   bar chart.

20) 126   (1 mark)
   Note to parent – Your child will probably partition
   each number into tens and units, then add all the
   tens and all the units. 30 + 50 + 30 = 110,
   4 + 7 + 5 = 16, 110 + 16 = 126. Encourage your
   child to play games where scores need to be
   added – e.g. darts, cards and board games.

21) £35   (1 mark)
   Note to parent – This is a 2-step problem, first
   involving multiplication and then subtraction.
   Encourage your child to solve simple, real-life
   problems involving money when shopping and
   spending pocket money.

22) a) 4 packs   (1 mark)
   Note to parent – When solving real-life problems
   children need to understand the context and when
   to round up in division.
   b) 8:45   (1 mark)
   Note to parent – Encourage your child first to add
   on the hour, then the half hour, using an analogue
   clock to help understanding when adding times.

23) Divide by 2   (1 mark)
   Note to parent – Your child may also identify this as
   halving. Give your child a rule and a starting number
   for a sequence and see how far they can go.

24) 35 and 70   (1 mark)
   Note to parent – Numbers exactly divisible by 5
   are those which end in a 5 or 0.

25) 832   (1 mark)
   Note to parent – Your child may partition the
   numbers into hundreds, tens and units –
   e.g. 300 + 400 = 700, 70 + 50 = 120, 9 + 3 = 12;
   700 + 120 + 12 = 832. They may start from 453 on
   a number line, then add 300, then 70, then 9. It
   may be worth checking with your child's class
   teacher which method is most commonly used
   in school.

26) 300   (1 mark)
   Note to parent – Your child will need to calculate
   60×5 using known number facts. They may
   recognise that 10 is double 5 so the missing
   number should be half of 600.

27) 1100   (1 mark)
   Note to parent – This question requires an
   understanding of place value beyond 1000. When
   rounding to the nearest hundred any number above
   and including 50 rounds up to the next hundred.

Paper

A

KEY STAGE 1
Levels 1–2

Test Paper A

Maths

Test Paper A

Test Paper A

Instructions:

- find a quiet place where you can sit down and complete the test paper undisturbed

- an adult will need to read the first 5 questions to you

- make sure you have all the necessary equipment to complete the test paper (a pencil, rubber and ruler)

- read the questions carefully

- answer all the questions in this booklet

- go through and check your answers when you have finished the test paper

Time:

Take as long as necessary to complete the test paper.

Note to Parents:

Check how your child has done against the mark scheme in the Answers Booklet.

Test Paper A

Page	3	5	7	9	11	13	15	16	Max. Mark	**Actual Mark**
Score	....	....	....	....	....	....	....	....	30	30

First name

Last name

1 What number is 7 less than 15? **Write your answer in box a.**

2 There are 4 tables in the classroom. 5 children sit at each table. How many children are there altogether? **Write your answer in box b.**

3 Look at the shapes. All but one of the shapes are triangles. **Circle the shape that is not a triangle.**

4 Circle the sum that gives the answer 4.

5 Tick the scales which show $2\frac{1}{2}$ kg.

Now continue with the rest of the paper on your own.

1 a) | 8 | *(1 mark)* ☑
Q1

2 b) | 2 0 | *(1 mark)* ☑
Q2

3

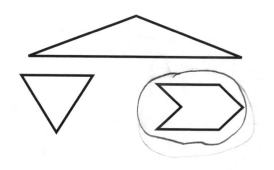

(1 mark) ☑
Q3

4 18 − 5   (20 ÷ 5)   4 + 2   4 × 4   *(1 mark)* ☑
Q4

5

☐   ☐   ☐   ☑

(1 mark) ☑
Q5

Turn over

subtotal

6 There are 8 stickers in Mia's book.

She adds another 6 stickers.

How many stickers does she have altogether?

 stickers

(1 mark)

7 Tick (✔) the shape with 2 **short** sides and 2 **long** sides.

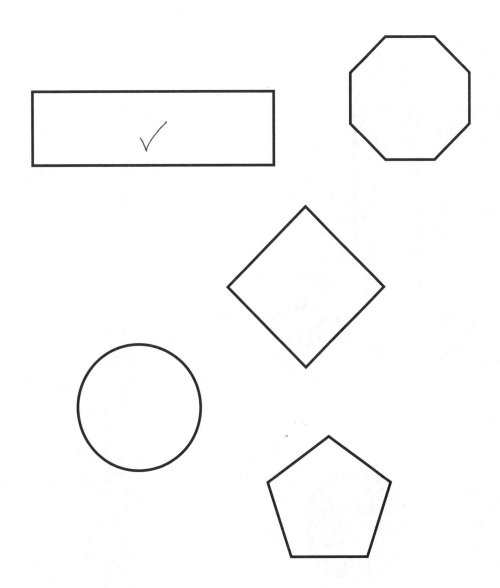

(1 mark)

8 Fill in 4 **different** missing numbers to make these sums correct.

a) $\boxed{7}$ + $\boxed{12}$ = 19   *(1 mark)*

b) 19 = $\boxed{18}$ + $\boxed{1}$ *(1 mark)*

Turn over

9   David wants to buy a carton of milk.

He has 15p.

How much **more** does he need?   8   p   *(1 mark)*

10   Write the answer.

8 + 4 + 7 + 3 =   22   *(1 mark)*

11 Write numbers in the boxes to make this sum correct.

| 2 | 3 | = | 3 | 7 | − | 1 | 4 |

(1 mark)

Q11

12 There are 10 satsumas in each bag and 7 more.

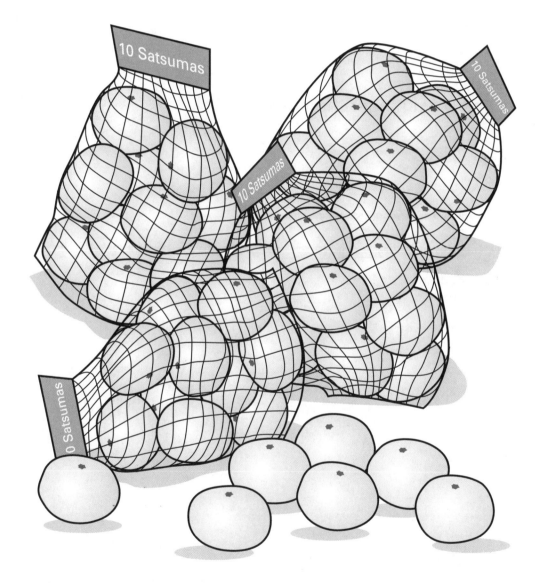

How many satsumas are there altogether?

| 4 7 | satsumas

(1 mark)

Q12

Turn over

subtotal

13 Write the missing numbers in the sequence.

54 49 44 39 34 29 24

(1 mark)

14 Draw a line 6 cm longer than this one.

Use a ruler.

(1 mark)

15 The 2 numbers joined together have a difference of 8.

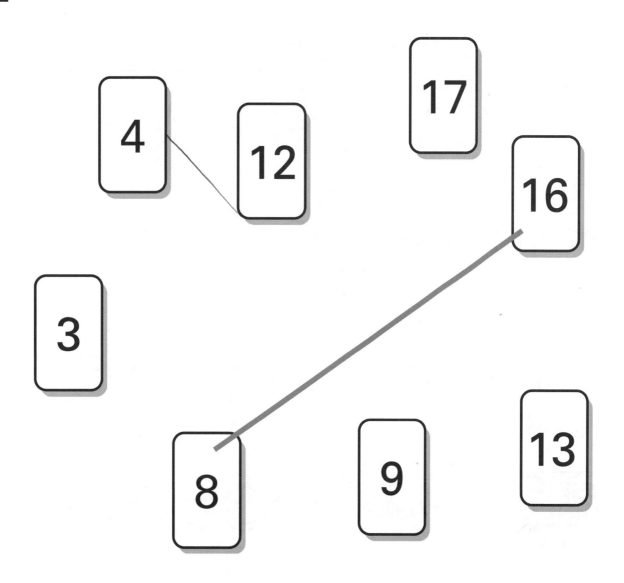

Join 2 other numbers together that have
a difference of 8.

(1 mark)

Q15

16 Some of these numbers can be divided exactly by 10.

12   (40)   35   28   (10)   36   (90)

Draw a circle round all the numbers which can be divided
exactly by 10.

(1 mark)

Q16

subtotal

17 Some children made a chart.

Our favourite playground game

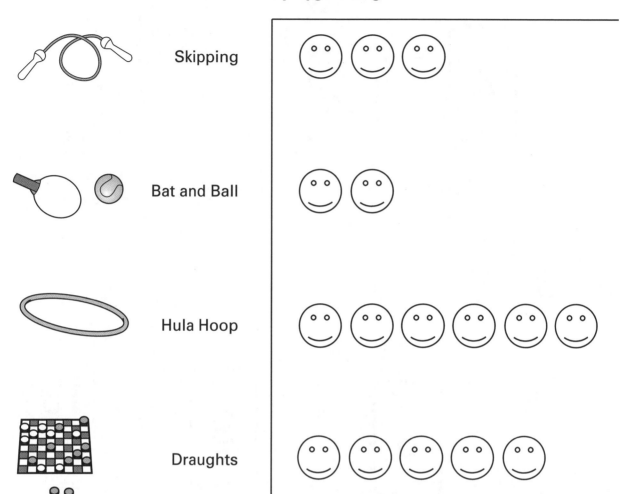

Skipping

Bat and Ball

Hula Hoop

Draughts

 **stands for** → **1 child**

How many more children chose
draughts than bat and ball?

$\boxed{3}$ children   *(1 mark)*

18 Put a ring round the **smallest** number.

108   199   198   (103)   133   183   *(1 mark)*

19

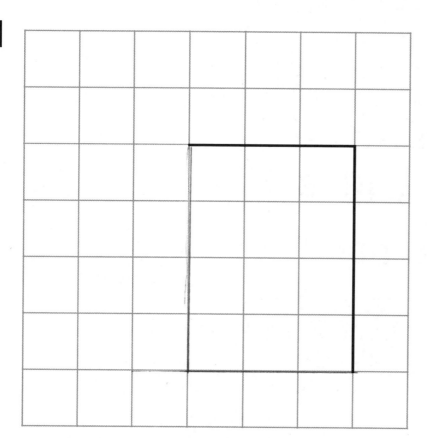

Draw the other 2 sides of this rectangle.

Use a ruler.   *(1 mark)*

20 James has 37p.

Marbles
5p each

a) How many marbles can he buy? 　7　 marbles 　*(1 mark)*

b) How much money will he have left? 　2　 p 　*(1 mark)*

21 Write the answer.

$$13 + 8 = 9 + \boxed{12}$$

(1 mark)

22 Joel scored 9 in a game of darts.

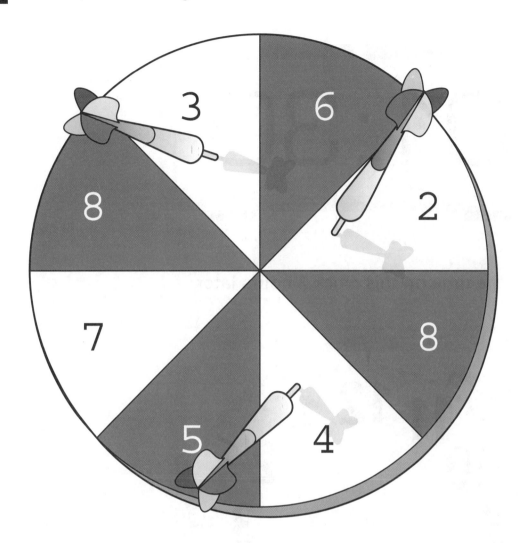

Chloe scored **double** Joel's score.

What score did Chloe get? | 18 | *(1 mark)* ☑

23 Complete the sequences.

a) 1   5   9 | 13 | 17 | 21 | 25   *(1 mark)* ☑

b) 26   22 | 18 | | 14 | 10 | 6 | 2   *(1 mark)* ☑

Turn over

24 Look at this clock.

Show the time on this clock 2 hours later.

(1 mark)

25 Write the number which is 12 **less than** 50.   38   *(1 mark)*

26 There are 25 people on a bus. At the next stop 8 people get off.

How many people are left on the bus?

| 17 | people

(1 mark)

Turn over

subtotal

27

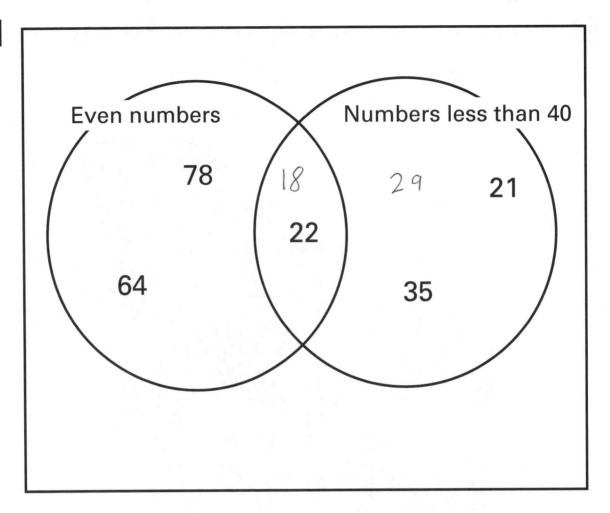

Even numbers

Numbers less than 40

78   18   29   21

22

64   35

Write these 2 numbers in the Venn diagram.

18   29

(1 mark)

END OF TEST

Paper
C

KEY STAGE 1
Level 3
Test Paper C

Maths

Test Paper C

Test Paper C

Instructions:

- find a quiet place where you can sit down and complete the test paper undisturbed

- an adult will need to read the first 5 questions to you

- make sure you have all the necessary equipment to complete the test paper (a pencil, rubber, ruler and small mirror)

- read the questions carefully

- answer all the questions in this booklet

- go through and check your answers when you have finished the test paper

Time:

Take as long as necessary to complete the test paper.

Note to Parents:

Check how your child has done against the mark scheme in the Answers Booklet.

Test Paper C

Page	3	5	7	9	11	13	15	17	19	Max. Mark	**Actual Mark**
Score	....	....	....	....	....	....	....	....	....	30	....

First name ....

Last name ....

Read out these questions carefully to your child. Explain that they should listen to you and then write the answers on the opposite page.

1 What is the total of 12, 9 and 6? **Write your answer in box a.**

2 A film starts at 6:30pm and finishes at 8:00pm.
How long does the film last? **Write your answer in box b.**

3 What is the difference between 65 and 42? **Write your answer in box c.**

4 Asif bought 3 packs of stickers at 15p each.
How much change did he get from 50p? **Write your answer in box d.**

5 Look at the shapes. **Circle the 2 shapes that have 4 right angles.**

Now continue with the rest of the paper on your own.

1 a) [rectangle] *(1 mark)* □
Q1

2 b) [rectangle] *(1 mark)* □
Q2

3 c) [rectangle] *(1 mark)* □
Q3

4 d) [rectangle] p *(1 mark)* □
Q4

5

(1 mark) □
Q5

Turn over

subtotal

6 Which number comes **halfway** between 420 and 520?

Write it in the box.

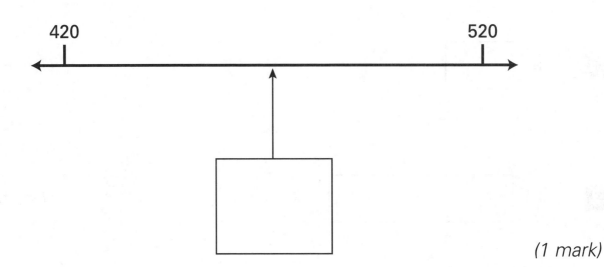

(1 mark)

7 Write the answer.

93 − 56 = ☐

(1 mark)

8 Draw lines to show where you would fold this shape to make a cube.

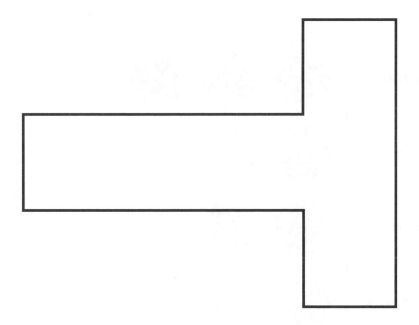

(1 mark)

9 Draw an arrow to show 750 g on the scale.

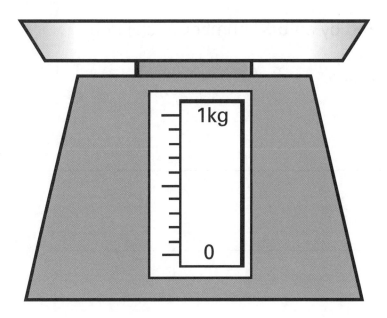

(1 mark)

Turn over

10 Look at the pictogram.

Favourite Pizza

Cheese and Tomato

Ham and Mushroom

Vegetarian

Seafood

Spicy Sausage

stands for 4 children

2 types of pizza are liked by an **odd** number of children.

a) Which pizzas are they?

_____

and _____ *(1 mark)*

b) How many children
   took part in this survey? [   ] children *(1 mark)*

11 Write these numbers in the circles.

All the numbers must be in order.

308   398   393

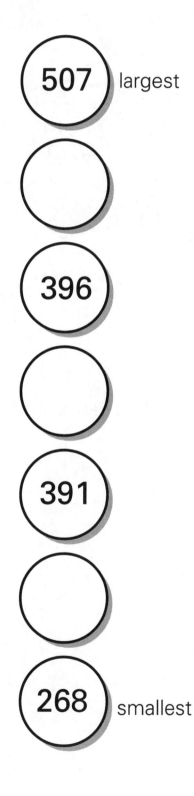

507) largest

396

391

268) smallest

(1 mark)

Q11

subtotal

How many centimetres had Paul's sunflower grown?

[   ] centimetres

(1 mark)

13 Draw 2 **lines of symmetry** on this shape. You may use a mirror.

(1 mark)

14 Sally is making a set of 4 wooden shelves. Each shelf is 80 cm long.

What length of wood does she need to buy? [　　　　] *(1 mark)*

Turn over

subtotal

15 Write the answer.

$\boxed{}$ = 90 ÷ 5

(1 mark)

16 Look at the digit cards.

Use all the digits to make the number nearest to 900.

(1 mark)

17 Circle the 2 numbers which total 70.

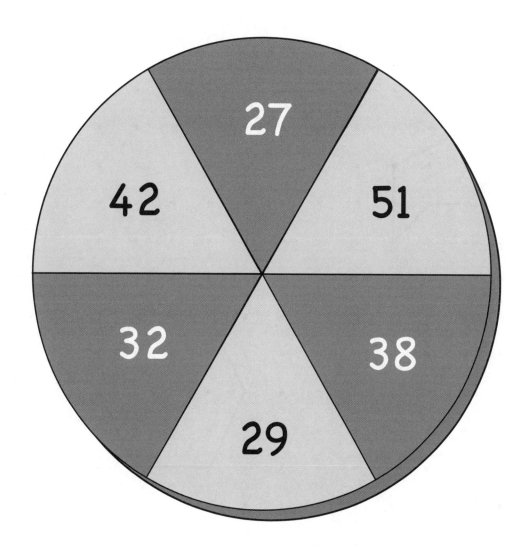

(1 mark)

18 Use the dots to draw a **different** hexagon.

Use a ruler.

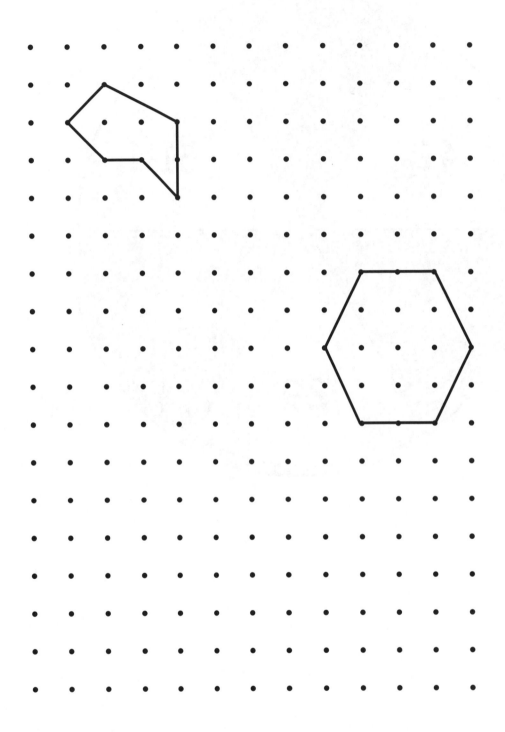

(1 mark)

Q1

19 Look at the bar chart.

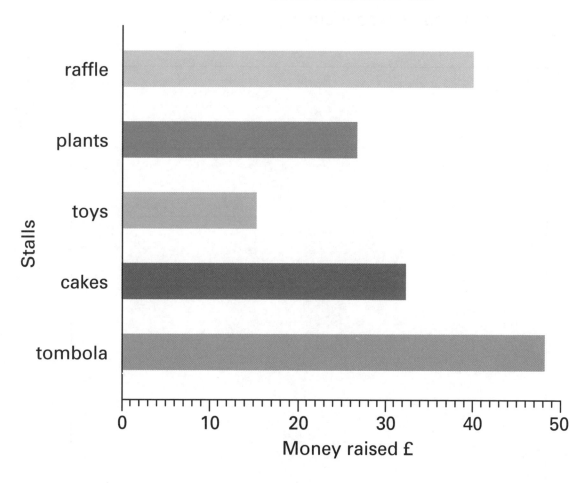

School summer fair

a) Which stalls raised between £25 and £35?

_____ and _____ *(1 mark)*

Q19a

b) How much money did the **tombola** raise?   £ [ ]   *(1 mark)*

Q19b

20 Add together 34, 57 and 35.

Show how you worked it out in the box.

(1 mark)

21 Jo saved £5 each week for 9 weeks.

She wants to buy a CD player for £80.

**How much more money
does she need to save?**   £ ⬚

(1 mark)

Q21

subtotal

22 Marvin needs 20 burgers for his barbecue.

Burgers come in packs of 6.

a) How many packs does he need to buy? ☐ packs *(1 mark)*

His barbecue starts at 7:15 and lasts for 1½ hours.

b) Circle the time it finishes.

7:45   9:00   8:15

8:45   9:30   *(1 mark)*

23 Look at this sequence.

224   112   56   28   14   7

Tick (✔) the rule for this sequence.

☐ divide by 3

☐ add 7

☐ subtract 10

☐ divide by 2

24 Put a ring round the 2 numbers which divide by 5 with no remainder.

25 Write the answer.

379 + 453 = ☐

Show how you worked it out in the box.

(1 mark)

26 Write the answer.

$$60 \times 5 = \boxed{}$$

(1 mark)

27 Write the correct number in the box.

1067   to the nearest 100 $\boxed{}$ *(1 mark)*

END OF TEST

subtotal